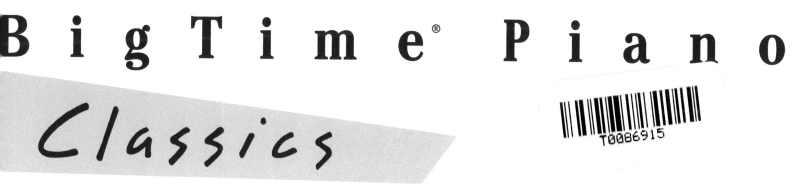

BigTime® Piano

Classics

Level 4 & above

Intermediate

This book belongs to: _____

Arranged by

Nancy and Randall Faber

Production Coordinator: Jon Ophoff
Design and Illustration: Terpstra Design, San Francisco
Engraving: Dovetree Productions, Inc.

FABER
PIANO ADVENTURES®
3042 Creek Drive
Ann Arbor, Michigan 48108

A NOTE TO TEACHERS

BigTime® Piano Classics is a treasury of the most popular and most requested masterworks of Western music. The selections are taken from original sources and arranged to be accessible to the intermediate pianist. Care has been taken to create a "big" sound while remaining within the level.

The *Classics* books are available in all levels of the *PreTime® to BigTime® Piano Supplementary Library*. They offer the piano student a wonderful opportunity to explore important orchestral and operatic works.

BigTime® Piano Classics is part of the *BigTime® Piano* series arranged by Faber and Faber. As the name implies, this level marks a point of significant achievement for the piano student. Following are the levels of the supplementary library which lead up to *BigTime®*.

PreTime® Piano	(Primer Level)
PlayTime® Piano	(Level 1)
ShowTime® Piano	(Level 2A)
ChordTime® Piano	(Level 2B)
FunTime® Piano	(Level 3A - 3B)
BigTime® Piano	(Level 4 - above)

Each level offers books in a variety of styles, making it possible for the teacher to offer stimulating material for every student. For a complimentary detailed listing, e-mail faber@pianoadventures.com or write us at the mailing address listed below.

Visit **www.PianoAdventures.com**.

Helpful Hints:

1. Pieces can be assigned in any order, according to the student's interest and enthusiasm.

2. Students should be encouraged to listen to recordings of the selections. This will enhance their conception and performance of the pieces while preparing them to be appreciative concertgoers.

3. Hands-alone practice can be used after the notes are learned to improve technique, tone, articulation, shape and listening skill.

About the Classics

A "classic" is a work of art or literature that is generally recognized to be of the highest quality. Many works of art were popular in their day, but later forgotten. A classic, however, withstands the test of time—it endures to be appreciated and enjoyed by later generations.

ISBN 978-1-61677-031-0

TABLE OF CONTENTS

4

Song of India
(from the opera *Sadko*)

Nicolai Rimsky-Korsakov
(1844-1908)

5

FF1031

Tales from the Vienna Woods
(Opus 325)

Johann Strauss, Jr.
(1825-1899)

Waltz tempo

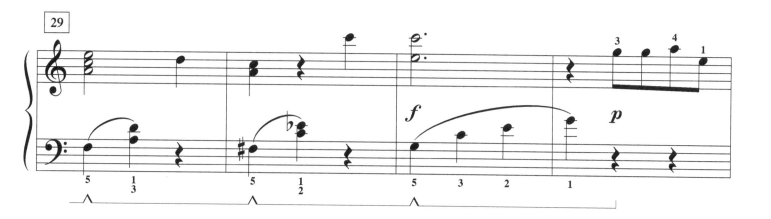

8

Habanera
(from the opera *Carmen*)

Georges Bizet
(1838-1875)

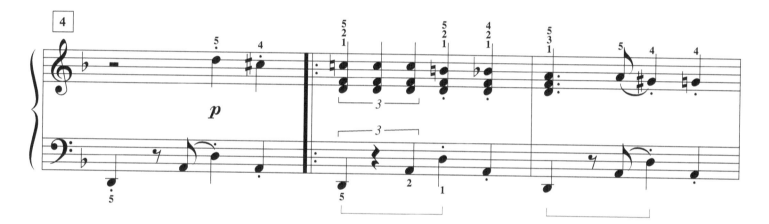

10

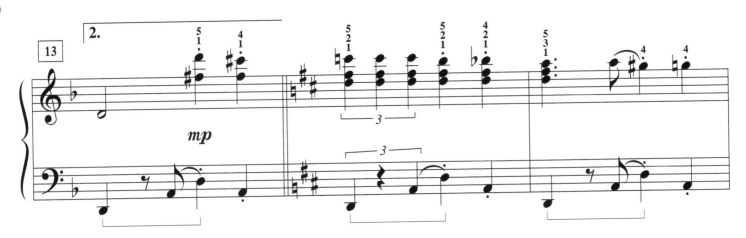

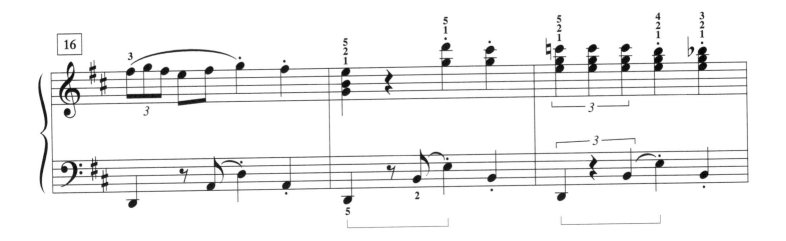

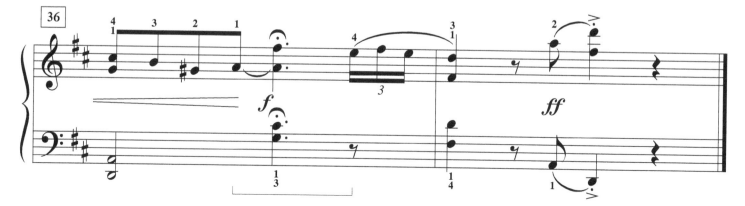

Hornpipe
(from *Water Music*)

George Frideric Handel
(1685-1759)

Moderato, with spirit

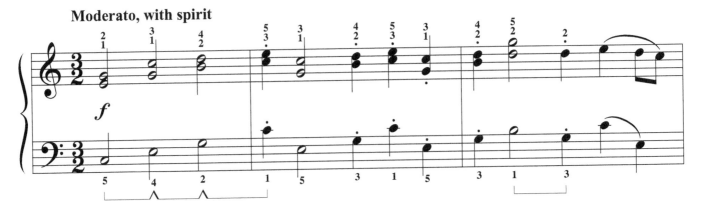

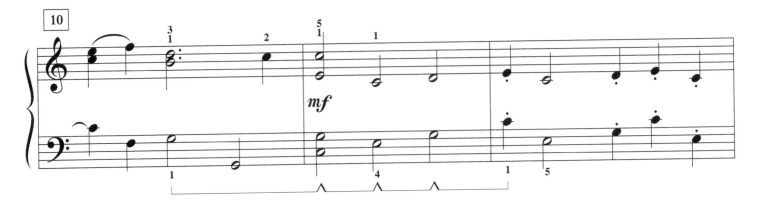

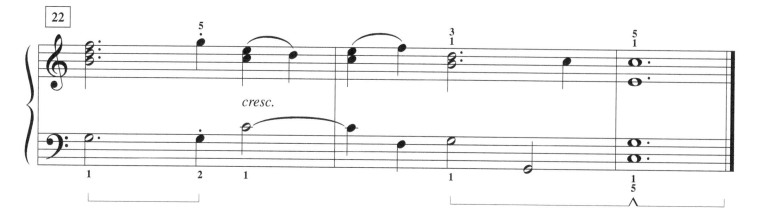

Arioso
(from *Cantata No. 156*)

Johann Sebastian Bach
(1685-1750)

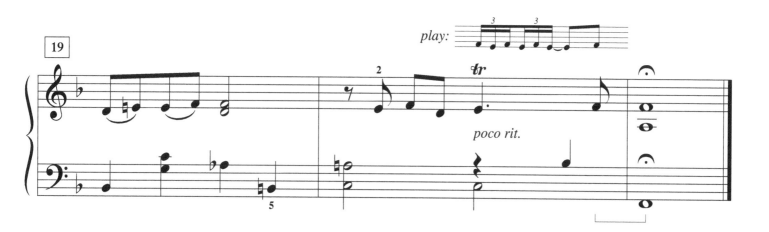

Hungarian Dance No. 5

Johannes Brahms
(1833-1897)

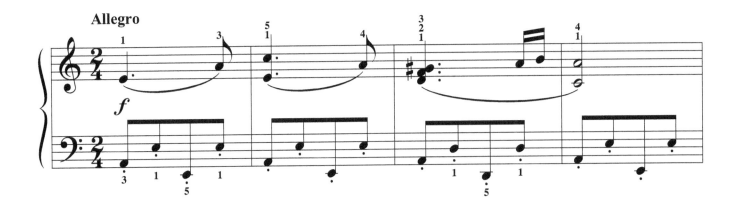

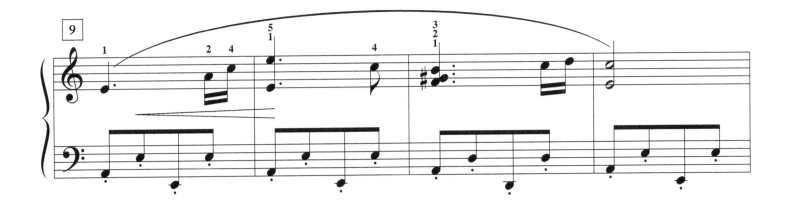

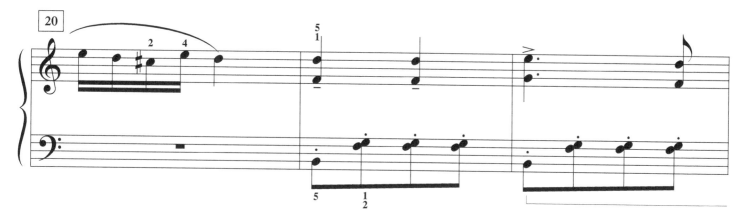

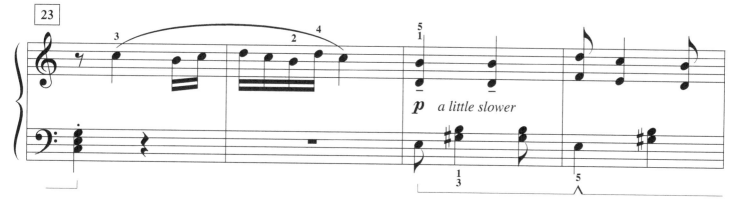

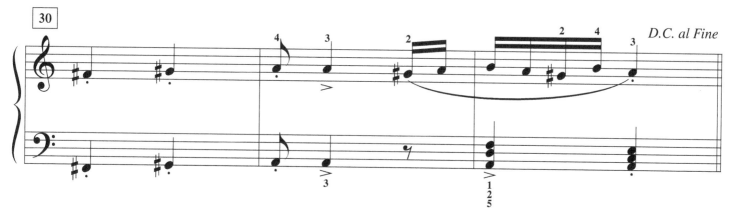

Canon in D

Johann Pachelbel
(1653-1706)

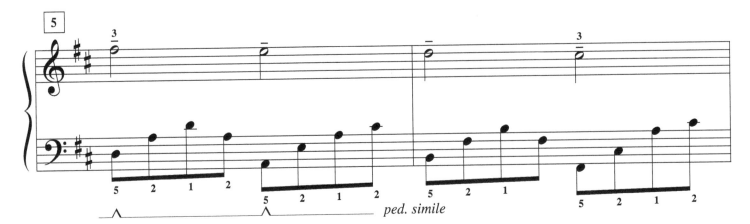

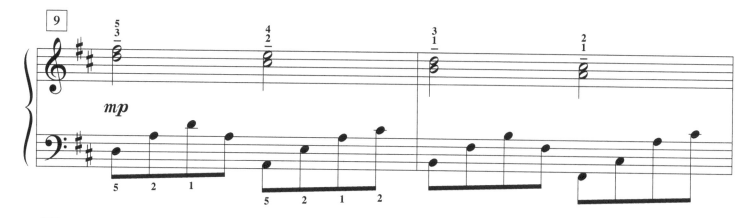

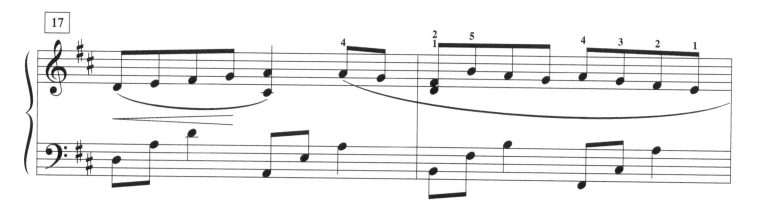

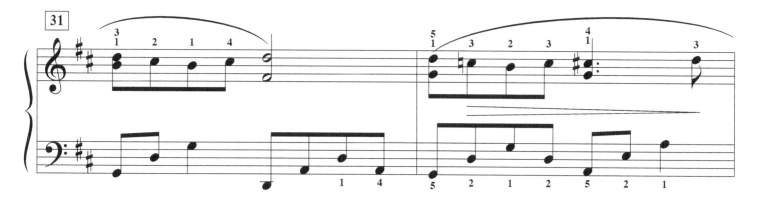

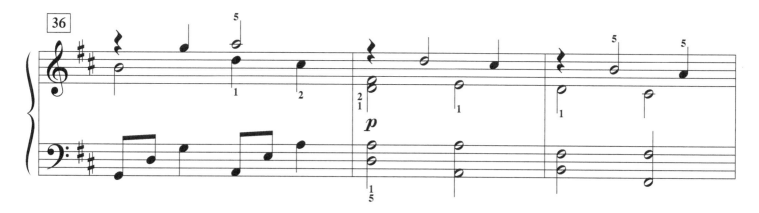

Rondeau
(from *Suite de Symphonies No. 1*)

Jean-Joseph Mouret
(1682-1738)

March tempo

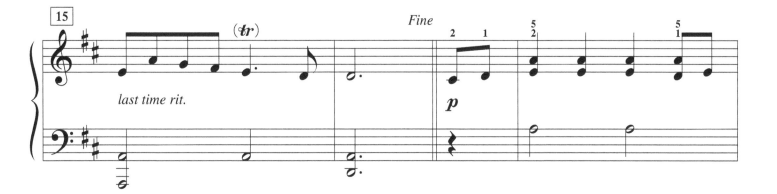

The Great Gate of Kiev
(from *Pictures at an Exhibition*)

Modest Mussorgsky
(1839-1881)

Maestoso

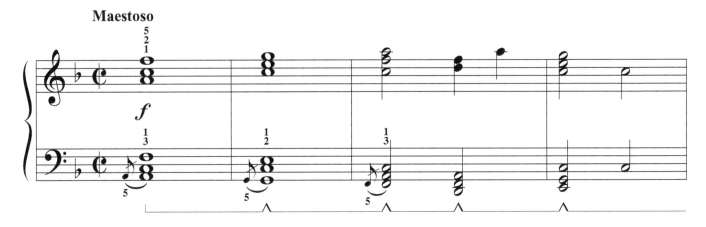

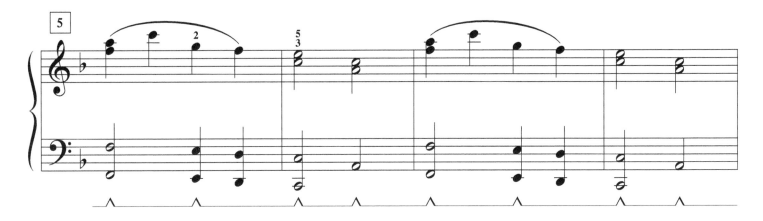

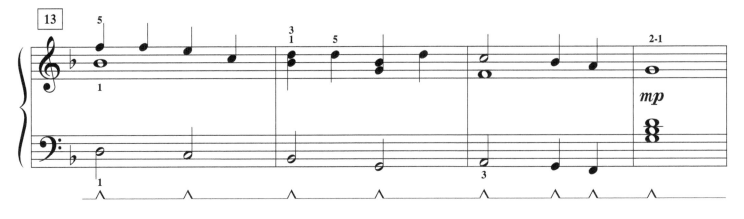

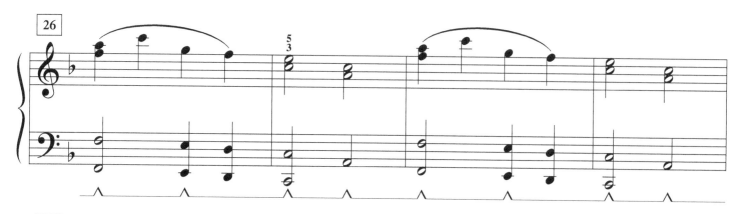

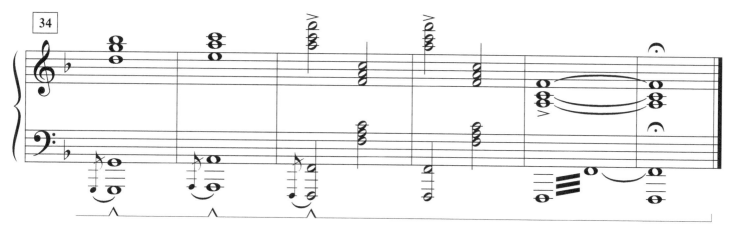

Spring Song

Felix Mendelssohn-Bartholdy
(1809-1847)

Allegretto

mp

mf

This arrangement © 1991 Dovetree Productions, Inc., c/o FABER PIANO ADVENTURES.
International Copyright Secured.   All Rights Reserved.

26

FF1031

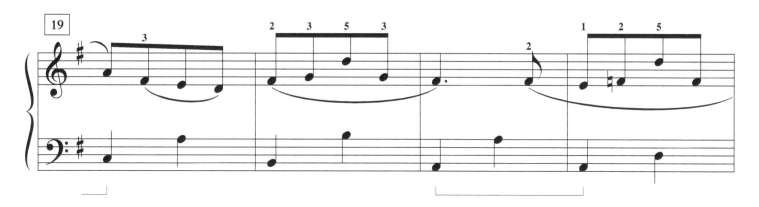

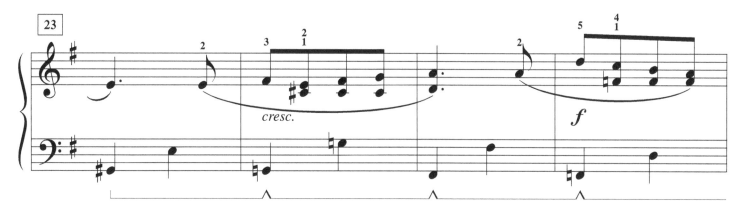

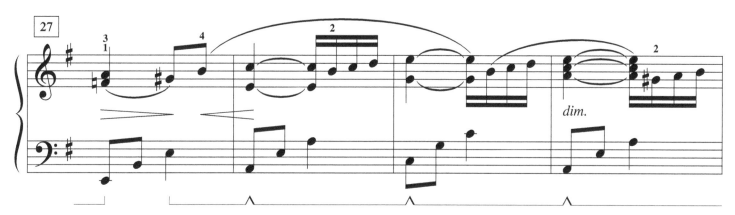

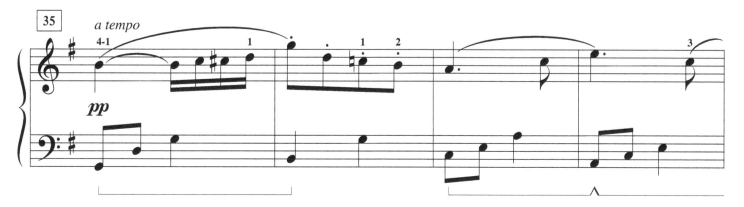

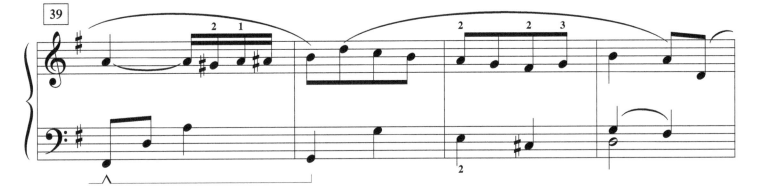

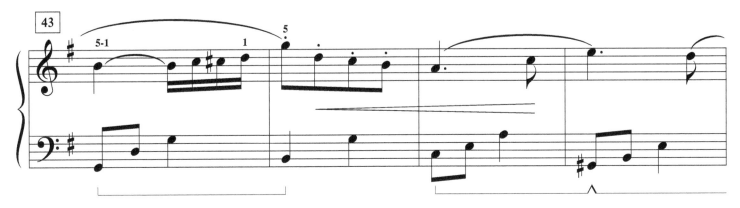

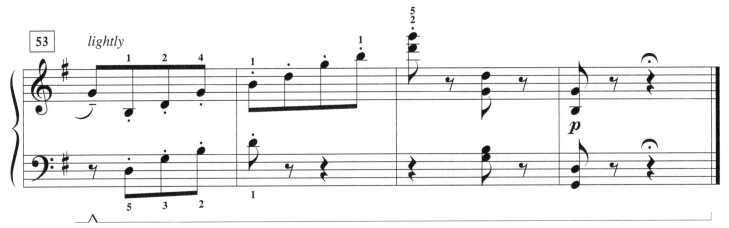

Theme from Symphony No. 40

Wolfgang Amadeus Mozart
(1756-1791)

Molto Allegro

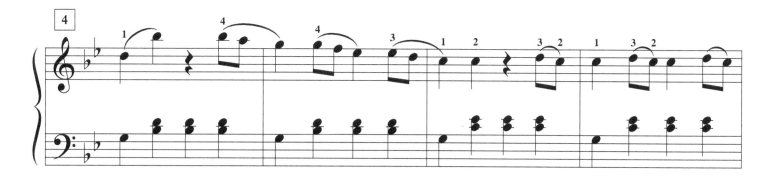

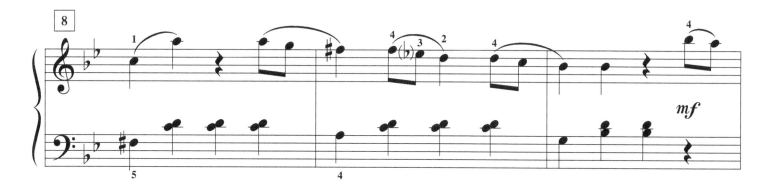

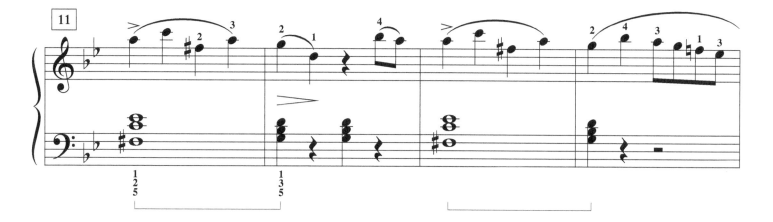

FF1031

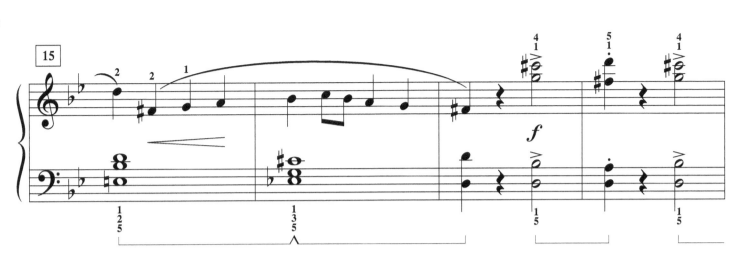

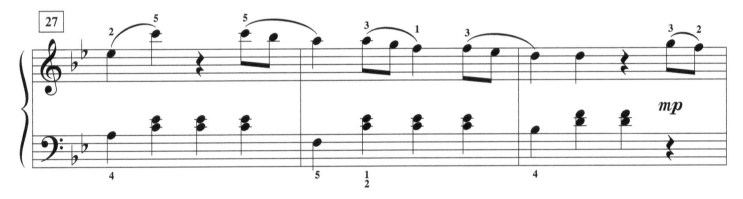

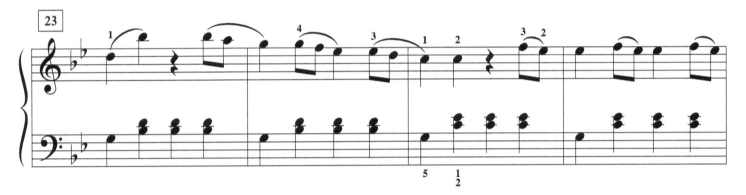

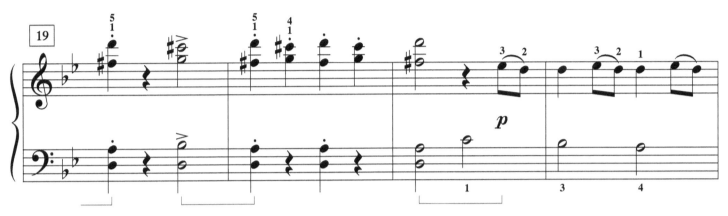

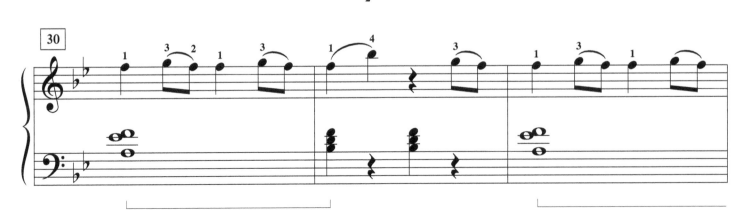

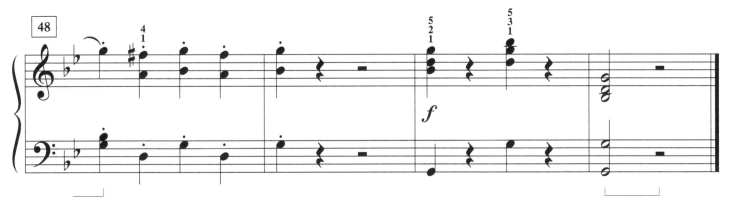

Russian Sailor's Dance
(from *The Red Poppy Ballet Suite,* Opus 70)

Reinhold Moritsevich Glière
(1875-1956)

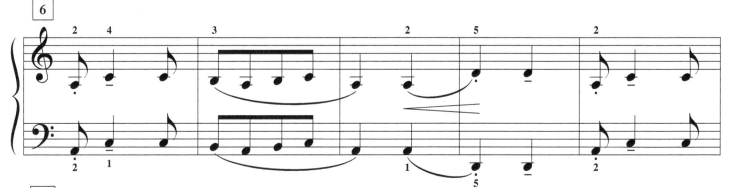

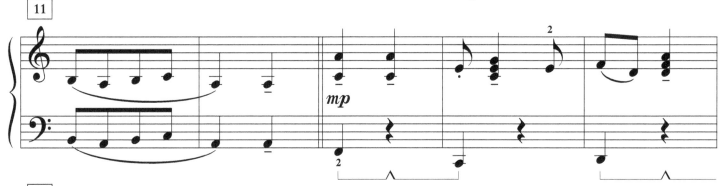

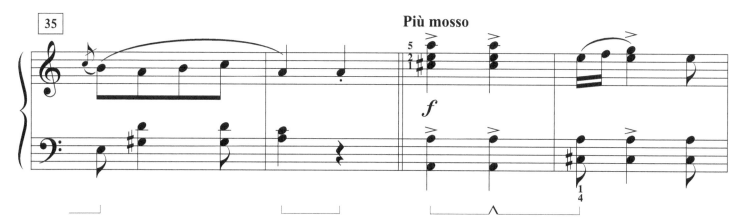

Danse Macabre

Camille Saint-Saëns
(1835-1921)

Spirited waltz tempo

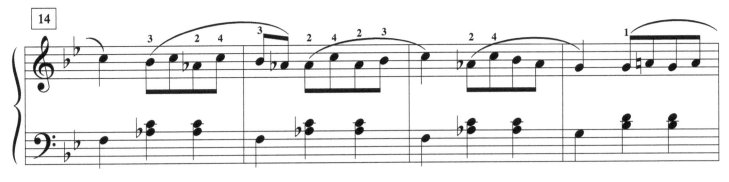

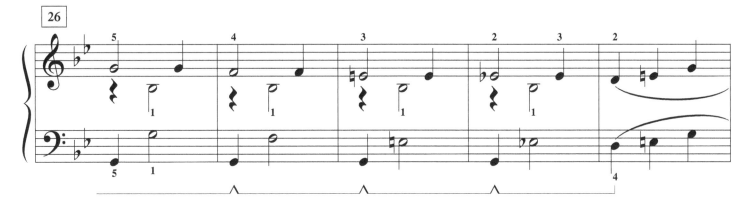

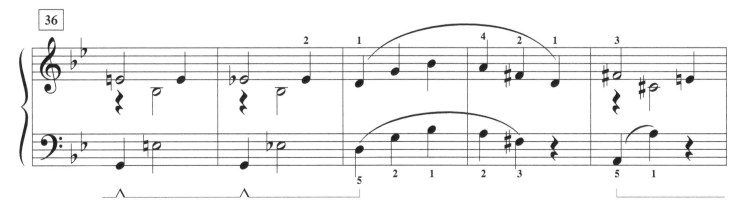

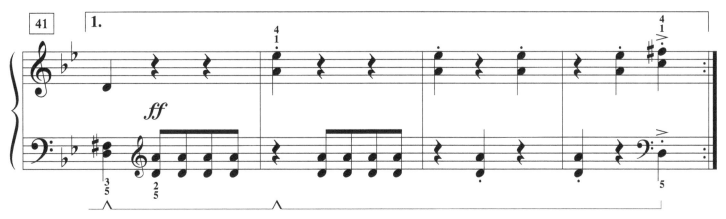

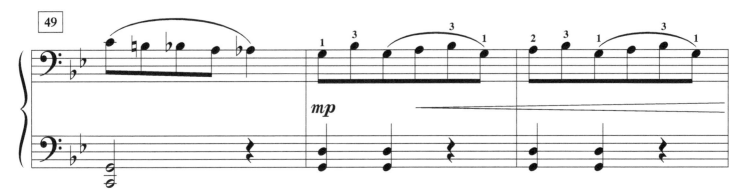

Liebesfreud

Fritz Kreisler
(1875-1962)

Graceful waltz tempo

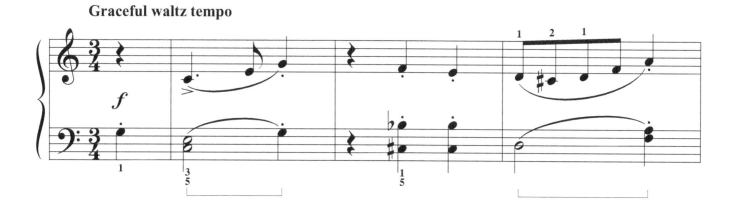

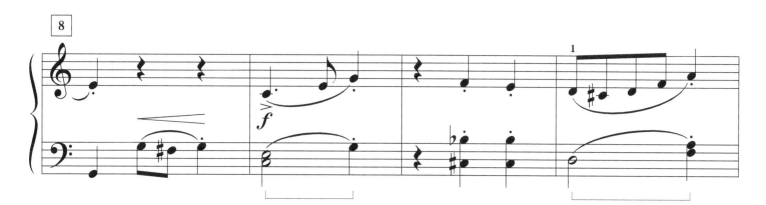

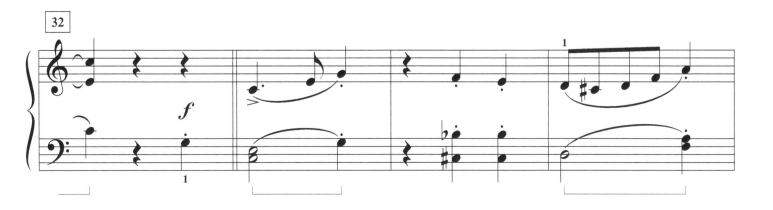

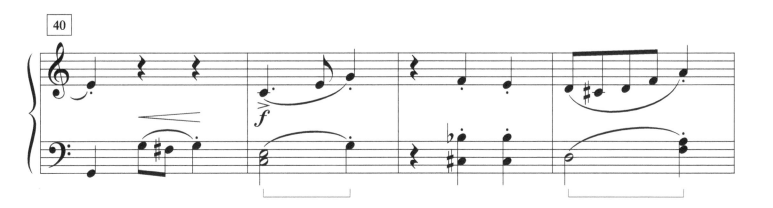

DICTIONARY OF CLASSICAL TERMS

Arioso "Like a song." A piece of instrumental music that has an expressive melody, as if written for voice. It should be played as if it were being sung.

Ballet Musical theater which uses dance to tell a story. Besides dance, ballet uses music, scenery and costumes (but no singing).

Canon A canon is a piece in which several players play the same tune, but enter at different times. The melody to Pachelbel's canon was originally played in this manner by three violins (similar to singing *Row, Row, Row Your Boat* in a "round"). The violins were accompanied by harpsichord and cello playing the bass line.

Cantata A large-scale vocal work for chorus and soloists with orchestral accompaniment. A cantata consists of a number of movements (related pieces) which are based on a continuous narrative text.

Habanera A dance from Cuba based on the rhythm ♫ ♩ ♪ ♩, the habanera is the ancestor of the tango. It was popular with French composers of the 1800's.

Opera A drama set to music, with singing, acting and, sometimes, dancing. In an opera, the characters express themselves by singing instead of speaking.

Song A short composition for voice, usually with accompaniment.

Suite A set of short pieces, often written in dance forms.

Symphony A major composition for symphony orchestra. A symphony usually has four movements (major sections).